PREFACE TO BONHOEFFER

Preface to Bonhoeffer

The Man and Two of His Shorter Writings

by John D. Godsey

FORTRESS PRESS   •   PHILADELPHIA

Translated from *Dein Reich Komme,*
edited by Eberhard Bethge,
Hamburg, Furche Verlag, 1957

Library of Congress Cataloging in Publication Data

Godsey, John D
    Preface to Bonhoeffer.

    Bibliography: p.
    CONTENTS: Bonhoeffer the man.—Thy kingdom come.—The first table of the Ten commandments.
    1. Kingdom of God.   2. God—Worship and love.   3. Commandments, Ten.   4. Bonhoeffer, Dietrich, 1906–1945.   I. Bonhoeffer, Dietrich, 1906–1945. Dein Reich komme. English. 1979. II. Bonhoeffer, Dietrich, 1906–1945. The first table of the Ten commandments. 1979.   III. Title.
BT94.G64 1979   231'.7   79–7378
ISBN 0–8006–1367–8   ----------------

First paperback edition 1979

7699C79   Printed in the United States of America   1–1367

CONTENTS

BONHOEFFER THE MAN

Why Dietrich Bonhoeffer? Why should English-speaking people read the writings of this German theologian with the rather formidable sounding name? And, in particular, why read these two essays entitled "Thy Kingdom Come" and "The First Table of the Ten Commandments"? For old acquaintances of Bonhoeffer's writings, who have long since come to appreciate their power and profundity, these are of course superfluous questions. But, then, introductions are not written for the initiated, and here it is our purpose to help those who have never heard of Bonhoeffer, or who have only a nominal acquaintance with him, to learn something about the man, his work, and his significance.

A SKETCH OF BONHOEFFER'S LIFE

First of all, who is Dietrich Bonhoeffer? What are the pertinent facts about his life and death? Let us begin at the beginning. Dietrich Bonhoeffer, along with a twin sister, was born in Breslau, Germany, on February 4, 1906, one of the eight children of Karl Ludwig and Paula (nee von Hase) Bonhoeffer. When he was six years old, the family moved to Berlin. There his father, a prominent neurologist, became the occupant of the first chair of psychiatry at the University of Berlin. Ten years later this young man, blessed with the educational and cultural advantages of middle class life in a Berlin suburb, decided to enter the ministry of the church.

Lutheran in background, Bonhoeffer was a member of the Prussian church, in which Lutheran and Reformed elements had united during the nineteenth century. He pursued his theological education briefly at Tübingen, but for the most part he studied at the university in his home city of Berlin. In 1927, when only twenty-one years old, he completed a doctoral dissertation entitled *Sanctorum Communio,* which was a perceptive theological inquiry into the sociology of the church. By 1930, after his one-year internship in a German-speaking congregation in Barcelona, Spain, he had finished a second dissertation, *Act and Being,* which won him the privilege of lecturing in the field of Systematic Theology at the University of Berlin. Before beginning this task, however, he took advantage of an opportunity to spend the 1930-31 academic year in the United States as Sloane Fellow at Union Theological Seminary in New York City, where he not only showed genuine interest in American theology and church life, but also helped interpret for Americans the then-dominant Continental theology of Karl Barth and his friends, with whose position Bonhoeffer broadly identified himself.

After his return to Berlin in 1931, Bonhoeffer began his lecturing as a *Privatdozent* at the University, but at the same time he accepted the responsibility for three other positions: chaplain to students at one of Berlin's technical colleges, leader of a confirmation class for a group of boys from a slum area, and Secretary of the Youth Commission of the World Alliance for International Friendship through the Churches and of the Universal Christian Council for Life and Work. Teacher, preacher, pastor, churchman—these are the concerns and capabilities evident throughout Bonhoeffer's career. The fruit of one of his lecture series, an exposition of the first three chapters of Genesis, was published in 1933 under the title, *Creation and Fall.* These numerous activities came to an abrupt end, however, in the autumn of 1933, when Bonhoeffer left Germany in protest against Adolf Hitler's Nazi regime and its deleterious (especially anti-Semitic) influence upon the church. He became pastor of two small German-speaking congregations in London, and from there he kept in close contact with developments in his homeland and also acted as a valuable interpreter of the real meaning of the German church struggle to the outside world.

In 1935 the leaders of the Confessing Church, that is, that body of Christians who took a firm, clear stand against the Nazi-influenced Reich Church and who claimed to be the true church of God in Germany, asked the talented twenty-nine-year-old pastor-theologian to return to Germany to establish and direct a clandestine seminary for their ministerial candidates. Although it meant giving up cherished plans for a trip to India to meet Gandhi and to study his non-violent method of resistance, Bonhoeffer responded to the call and set up a seminary at Finkenwalde near Stettin, where he led students not only in their academic studies, but also in the discipline of prayer and meditation on Holy Scripture. And perhaps we should mention dishwashing and singing around the piano in the evenings! This unusual school was first closed down by the Gestapo in 1937, but managed to continue on a makeshift basis until its final disruption in 1940. It was during these years that Bonhoeffer published two renowned books: *The Cost of Discipleship* (1937) and *Life Together* (1939).

An event in 1939 clearly indicates the mettle of the man. In the spring of that year some of Bonhoeffer's American friends, worried because they knew he faced military conscription and wishing to extricate him from the deteriorating situation in Germany, made arrangements for him to be invited to lecture in the United

States. The leaders of the Confessing Church urged him to accept the opportunity, and, with some reluctance, Bonhoeffer made his second trip to America, returning to Union Theological Seminary in New York. He had hardly set foot on the safe American shore, however, before his conscience told him he had made a wrong decision. A letter soon arrived from Germany with the news that war was imminent, and he forthwith returned to his homeland to live through the catastrophe with his people. The news was accurate. World War II erupted in September.

Twice, then, Bonhoeffer gave up the safety of foreign shores and returned to serve the needs of his people in Germany, but the second homecoming was to lead to consequences no one would have dared predict. With the outbreak of war and the disbandment of all seminary activity, Bonhoeffer entered what he called "the great masquerade of evil." Long before barred from his academic post at the University, and now prohibited by the Nazis from preaching or publishing or from even residing in Berlin, he joined, through the help of a brother-in-law, an underground resistance movement dedicated to the overthrow of Hitler's maniacal military dictatorship and to the re-establishment of peace. This decision meant becoming a civilian employee of the German Military Intelligence Service, the headquarters of which served as the nerve center of resistance activities. He was officially stationed in the Munich office, but was frequently called back to Berlin. Until his arrest on April 5, 1943, Bonhoeffer engaged in all kinds of ecclesio-political action, even making daring and dangerous trips to Switzerland and Sweden to contact Allied officials about possible peace terms. During this period he worked from time to time on his *Ethics,* a book he considered to be his life work. Unfortunately, he left behind only fragments, which were later collated and published posthumously in 1949.

Bonhoeffer spent most of his imprisonment in Berlin's Tegel Military Prison, where he was held on charges of suspicion which were not validated until after the unsuccessful attempt of Hitler's life on July 20, 1944. Through friendly orderlies he was able to carry on extensive uncensored correspondence with his parents and his fiancée, and also with his fellow pastor, teacher, and closest friend, Eberhard Bethge. Especially in letters to the latter he discussed his seminal and provocative reflections upon the state of Christianity and the meaning of Christ for our modern world. These letters, written from a solitary prison cell, have made a remarkable impact on the world, particularly the world of theologians and churchmen, since their posthumous publication in 1951. The English publication is entitled *Letters and Papers from Prison;* the American, *Prisoner for God.*

In September, 1944, the Gestapo discovered papers that linked Bonhoeffer to the resistance movement, and soon thereafter he was moved from Tegel to the infamous Gestapo prison in Prinz Albrecht Strasse. In February, 1945, he was transferred from Berlin to the concentration camp at Buchenwald and, finally, in accordance with one of Hitler's last diabolical orders, he was executed at Flossenbürg, a Gestapo camp in southern Germany, on April 9, 1945, only days before the camp was liberated by the advancing American army.

Two years of prison and then death at the age of thirty-nine—these events are the unexpected conclusion of the amazingly rich and fruitful life of Dietrich Bonhoeffer, whose story, as his friend Reinhold Niebuhr has aptly remarked, belongs to the modern Acts of the Apostles.

WHY BONHOEFFER IS SIGNIFICANT

It is precarious to try to assess the significance of any man, particularly when we live in the same era and do not have the advantage of the "judgment of history." Nevertheless, we are faced with the fact that the witness of Dietrich Bonhoeffer, his life and his writings, is exerting an extraordinary influence on contemporary Christians, not to speak of many people who never darken the door of the church. Moreover, his influence cuts across our customary theological, denominational, national, and age-group divisions. Bonhoeffer has long been avidly read by seminary and college students, but now it is not at all surprising to find one of his books being used as a text for study groups in local congregations. What has struck a responsive chord? Why is Bonhoeffer so significant? We would like to propose a few reasons for his impact on the world today.

1. *Bonhoeffer understands our world.* To a remark-

able degree this young man caught the spirit of our age, the mood of our time, and we instinctively feel that we can identify ourselves with him because he has identified himself with us. Ours is a restless and rootless generation that knows the terror and the awe of stupendous technological and scientific achievement. It knows man's potential for good, but it also knows the magnitude of evil and man's capacity for corruption, self-deception, and inhumanity. We are aware of both our grandeur and our misery. Our world is in flux at all levels, and the one thing certain is that nothing is certain, nothing stays the same. Well, almost nothing. We do believe that the sun will rise each morning, but that with it will inevitably come new problems to be solved. We are never without our problems, but we no longer look beyond the horizon of history for their solution. And we also find our enjoyments, and in spite of everything, we look forward to experiencing more joys along life's way—but never without problems. Even though our "one world" is fast diminishing in size, its complexities and perplexities seem to grow at an inverse ratio. Moreover, we have no illusions that the exploration of space will basically change things, just as the discovery of nuclear power did not. Joy and sorrow, pleasure and problems—we expect nothing else.

How do we face our problems? We put our brains to work with the best scientific or technical knowledge at our disposal, or we use the trial and error method, or just plain common sense. Where we can learn from the past, we do so; but we are never beholden to it. We focus our attention on the present, and sometimes, when we are at our best, we think of our responsibility for the future. But coping with the present is usually sufficient for the day, and our tendency is to sandwich in as many of life's pleasures as we can. Travel, theater, the arts, music, sports, hobbies, adventure—they all, or almost all, seem within our reach; and we genuinely hope they will soon be within the reach of all. Oh, we never forget that we have problems, world-wide and local and personal, but we rarely look upon them as insuperable. We only know that as soon as one is solved, there will be another in its place. Even our "boundary-situations"—sickness, suffering, guilt, death, and so on—do not bother us too much; we insure ourselves against them as well as possible and let it go at that, because they lie on the periphery of our normal existence. The pathos of the existentialists who breed on despair we find generally boring or incredible.

And what of religion? Granted that the term is difficult to define, a fact which in itself should give us pause, it is evident that our talk of "religious revival" is shallow indeed. For the most part, our religion is a mask which covers a thoroughgoing secularity; indeed, our affirmation of a "Supreme Deity" has as little consequence for our lives as the communist's denial of the same, which means that the communist is more honest with himself. We can still speak of "God," of course, and that all too easily; but "God" more often than not turns out to be a mere

9

symbol we use to complete our world-view or to meet our personal needs in the boundary situations of life or to "save our souls" for a world beyond. That is, "God" is still a convenient crutch for many people, but this crutch is becoming more and more anachronistic in our world. A nineteenth-century philosopher, Friedrich Nietzsche, sounded the death knell for this "God" that man uses, declaring "God is dead." This use of religion is true for all of us, whether we want to admit it or not. The philosophical "God" of classical metaphysics, the pietistic "God" of inwardness, the otherworldly "God" of Protestant orthodoxy—these "Gods" cut little ice today. When religious institutions do become meaningful for us, it is either when they enter helpfully into the common process of problem solving or—and we say this advisedly—when they confront us with the true God. The true God! Aha, you say, now we are back to "religion," albeit the "true religion" that stands over against all religiosity and all secularity as well. But does this necessarily follow? Could it be that the true God is the God who has become, dare we say, secular, and who thereby affirms the secular against all religion—and does so because it is *his* world, the world he has created, preserved, set subject to laws, reconciled, and made new?

If this brief description of our world is at all accurate, if we actually live according to reason-discovered laws that would still be true *etsi deus non daretur,* even if there were no God, then we repeat that Bonhoeffer caught its spirit and discerned its mood. To depict our modern world he coined the catch-word, ''world come of age,'' by which he meant that we have become adult in the sense that we rightly refuse to fall prey to any religion that tries to make man dependent on things on which he in fact is no longer dependent or to thrust problems on him which in fact are no longer problems for him or to exploit his weaknesses for purposes alien to him and not freely subscribed to by him. There can be no return to the domination of the medieval church, no more clericalism, no more separation of God from the world, no more division of the world into two spheres, one sacred and the other secular. And the surprising thing about Bonhoeffer's advocation of an adult world—and we must caution against the mistaken notion that ''adult'' means ''sinless'' or ''perfect''—is that he does it on christological grounds. That is, Bonhoeffer believes it is God's will, revealed in Jesus Christ, that has forced the world to become mature, that has forced man to recognize the de-divinization of the world and its gods, that has called man to an acceptance of his free and autonomous responsibility for the world. In short, it is God himself who demands that we be ''worldly.'' And this idea brings us to our second point.

2. *Bonhoeffer discerns the universal meaning of Jesus Christ.* Some theologians think that a Christ-centered theology does not do justice to the Triune God, who is ''much more.'' They are particularly disturbed by the lack of emphasis on the Father, who as the Creator supposedly

makes himself known through the orders of creation, and on the Holy Spirit, who as the Illuminator, Comforter, and Sanctifier supposedly makes himself known in the hearts of men. What they fail to realize is that they have fallen into a tri-theism that violates the generally accepted ground rule of the doctrine of the Trinity, namely, "The works of the Trinity in relation to the creation are undivided." Furthermore, in appealing to a knowledge of God apart from Jesus Christ they disregard the blindness of sinful man to true reality and actually advocate a "God" who is no more than an extension of the world. It was Bonhoeffer's contention, and we think he was right, that in the man Jesus Christ all that is to be known of God in his relation to the world is revealed. We know God only in this human form, in the "incognito" of the flesh, in the weakness of the crib and the cross, in the One whose entire concern was for others—even unto death. But precisely in him we know all.

What do we mean by "all"? Just this: that through and in him all reality, the reality of the world and the reality of God, is opened up to us. Or as Bonhoeffer put it: the more exclusively we hold to Jesus Christ as Lord, the more do we see the extensiveness of his dominion. Christ is Lord of all: Lord of the church and Lord of the world. In him God has reconciled the world to himself, as the Apostle Paul said long ago, and Bonhoeffer emphasized that this fact means that we can never have God without the world or the world without God. In Jesus

Christ God and the world are held together in a "polemical" unity that denies both deistic separation and pantheistic identification, and also disallows those oft-used divisions between the sacred and the secular, the revelational and the rational, the supernatural and the natural, the Christian and the worldly. It is not that these distinctions are not meaningful, but that because of the unity derived from the reality of Christ, they never assume a static independence. Rather, just as in Christ the reality of God entered the reality of the world, so the sacred is to be found only in the secular, the revelational only in the rational, the supernatural only in the natural, the Christian only in the worldly. It is precisely for this reason that the Christian cannot withdraw from the world, but through Christ is led to the world and yet sees the world in true perspective, that is, in the light of the Incarnate One, the Crucified One, and the Risen One.

What does it mean that Jesus Christ is the incarnate God? For Bonhoeffer it means that God loves his creation, that he wishes to exist "for us" rather than for himself, that he enters into created reality, indeed, that he takes upon himself bodily all human being and can henceforth be found only in human form. It means, too, that no created thing or person can be understood without reference to Christ, the Mediator of creation, and that man is made free to be really man before God, to exist not for himself but for God and other men. That Jesus Christ is the crucified Reconciler means at once God's condemnation of the fallen creation which has become godless and yet his mercy in freely reconciling this world to himself and setting man free for a life before God of genuine worldliness in the midst of the godless world. That Jesus Christ is the risen Lord means, according to Bonhoeffer, that he has overcome sin and death and has called new life into being and that he is the living Lord of all creation, a lordship that is not alien to creation, since all things were created through and for him and find their goal in him. It is Christ who sets creation free to fulfil its own law, that is, the law inherent in it by virtue of its having its origin, goal, and essence in him. From this standpoint Bonhoeffer is able to open up for Protestant ethics the whole neglected realm of the ''natural,'' which he defines as that which after the fall is open to Christ, as well as the realm of the ''things before the last,'' the penultimate affairs of life involving such things as food, health, education, and so forth, that have their legitimation from their connection with the ''last things,'' God's ultimate word of justification by grace and faith alone.

When Bonhoeffer asks in his letters from prison how we can speak of God without religion, how we can speak of him in a worldly sense, he does so because of his conviction that Jesus Christ is not an object to religion, but in truth the Lord of the world. God is transcendent, but this is an ethical, not an epistemological, transcendence. God is the ''beyond'' in the midst of our life, not the ''be-

14

yond'' of otherworldly religions, with their myths of salvation. God's being is disclosed in Jesus' being-there-for-
others, in his deputyship, in his suffering love. Man's religiosity, claims Bonhoeffer, makes him use God as a *deus*
ex machina, a power he can call on in time of distress,
but the biblical God is one who conquers the world by
his weakness, the Crucified One. If we really want to be
''honest to God,'' then our question must be: Who is
Jesus Christ for us today? This is the question Bonhoeffer
has put to the church. Only ultimate honesty in answering
this question will save the church from irrelevance; Bonhoeffer's insistence that Jesus, the man for others, does not
separate us from reality precisely because all reality is
christologically structured seems to us to lead in the right
direction. But this idea raises the question of what it
really means to be a Christian, to be a member of the
church, which brings us to our next point.

3. *Bonhoeffer recalls the church to discipleship.* Some
people look upon Bonhoeffer's books such as *The Cost of*
Discipleship and *Life Together* as inimical to the ''Christian worldliness'' of the letters from prison. In our opin-
ion, nothing could be further from the truth. Only the
disciplined disciple who learns the cost of following Jesus
attains the goal of a genuinely worldly life. Of course, it
would be possible to misunderstand discipleship in such a
way that the initial breach with the world would lead to
a withdrawal from and even perhaps a despising of the
world; Bonhoeffer recognizes this possibility in one of his

letters. But this otherworldliness would be a *mis*understanding, for if one truly follows Christ, he will follow him into the midst of the world, into its depths, its trivialities, its bondages—because that is where Christ is.

The Word became flesh, dwelt among us, was rejected, died on a cross. The Word was Jesus, and this "becoming" was the costliness of grace, of revelation and reconciliation. The church is called to proclaim this gracious Word, to witness to God's revelation, to be an agent of reconciliation. Dare it attempt to fulfil its calling cheaply, when grace was so costly for God? When God spoke, he did not merely say words; he enacted his Word. When the church speaks, it cannot merely repeat words; it must live by them. The enormous tragedy of Protestantism is that it has thought it was "proclaiming the Word" solely by right preaching and proper administration of the sacraments, forgetting that its words and liturgy lack power if they are not validated by the life of the community, both in its gathered and in its scattered existence. Without discipleship, the church peddles what Bonhoeffer called "cheap grace." Through discipleship Christians can be genuinely worldly, because they can live in the midst of the world as those in whom the knowledge of death and resurrection is ever present. In this way the false worldliness of the godless world will not be glossed over, but exposed for what it is.

What is the church? This is a question with which Bonhoeffer wrestled from the beginning to the end of his career. Eberhard Bethge has pointed to Bonhoeffer's passion for the concrete, not only for the concretion of revelation but for the concretion of the church. He would have nothing to do with notions of invisibility, and it is characteristic that his doctoral dissertation had to do with the *sociology* of the communion of the saints. His favorite definition of the church at that time was "Christ existing as a community," and he understood it to be a community constituted by the presence of Christ in the Word, in the sacrament, and in the fellowship of faithful persons who live according to the principle of vicarious action, that is, an active "being for one another." In his *Ethics* Bonhoeffer speaks of the church as Christ's Body, which is not a religious community of worshipers of Christ, but rather Christ himself who has taken form among men. This form is the proper form of all humanity, and thus what takes place in the church takes place as an example and substitute for all men. On the one hand, the congregation stands as a deputy for the world, and, on the other, the world achieves its fulfilment in the congregation. But, stresses Bonhoeffer, the church stands in this twofold relationship wholly in the fellowship and discipleship of its Lord, who was Christ by virtue of his existence not for his own sake but entirely for the sake of the world. In an outline of a book sketched in prison Bonhoeffer is content to say that the church is its true self only when it exists for humanity.

Can anyone deny that our churches, which often resemble social clubs that champion their own interests, desperately need to hear Bonhoeffer's call to discipleship, to life together under the Word, to vicarious existence for the world in the world? Even a "theology of revelation" becomes perverse if it allows us to stand over against the world rather than leading us to responsible sharing in the problems and burdens of the world. The church has absolutely no cause for pride, because the message it proclaims is meant for all mankind. The real difference between Christians and unbelievers, declared Bonhoeffer, is that Christians range themselves with God in his suffering, participating in the suffering of God in the life of the godless world.

There is another important truth that our churches need to learn from Bonhoeffer, especially in this day when there is so much controversy over relations between church and state. We have seen how Bonhoeffer refuses to divide reality into two static spheres, one sacred (the church) and one secular (the world). Although church and world are united in Christ, they are united "polemically" and retain their distinctiveness. Their differences are not to be understood in static, spatial terms, but in terms of the divine commission that has been laid upon them. It was Bonhoeffer's belief that Scripture teaches that God has imposed four mandates upon the world, that is, upon all men, and that these are equally divine by virtue of their relation to Jesus Christ, in whom they have their origin and goal. These four are labor (sometimes "culture" was included here), marriage, government, and the church. None is divine in itself, but only insofar as it exists for the sake of Jesus Christ. None is superior to the other; each has its peculiar function in helping man participate in the reality of the will of God fulfilled in Jesus Christ. By labor and marriage man participates in God's creative power; government preserves what is created and keeps it in order; the church proclaims the Word of God and enables the reality of Jesus Christ to become real in the Christian's life, thus impinging on all the other mandates. That is, the laborer, the partner in marriage, and the subject of a government is called to be a Christian worker, husband, and citizen. Thus the mandates are not meant to divide man and cause endless conflicts, but rather to bring wholeness into his life before God. They function conjointly under the commandment of God revealed in Jesus Christ, which embraces the whole of life, namely, the permission to live as man before God.

When people complain that the government should permit or even foster prayer or Bible reading in public schools, should they not consider whether this properly belongs to the mandate of government? Or when Christians talk of "going into full-time Christian service," as if professional church work were somehow sacrosanct in comparison with other vocations, should they not be reminded that the mandates are equally "divine" in the eyes of God? The task of the church, Bonhoeffer insists, is to tell men, whatever their calling, what it means to live in

19

Christ, to exist for others. When the church itself again discovers what this life means, that is, when it again takes discipleship seriously, not only the clergy but particularly the laity will find that being Christian, which means being fully human, has radical implications for every area of life. It is not at all surprising, in fact, that Bonhoeffer's thought has been one of the chief catalysts in the recovery of a "theology of the laity" in our time.

4. *Bonhoeffer's life gives power to his words.* In an essay called "What Is Meant by 'Telling the Truth'?" Bonhoeffer speaks of words no longer possessing any weight because there is too much talk that is mere idle chatter and of words becoming rootless and homeless because they have lost any vital relationship to reality. In his *Ethics* he raises the question of the warrant for ethical discourse and asserts that timeless and placeless ethical discourse lacks the concrete validation which all authentic ethical discourse requires. The words may be correct, but they have no weight. In *Letters and Papers from Prison* Bonhoeffer speaks in one place of the church's having fought for self-preservation as though it were an end in itself, thereby losing its chance to speak a word of reconciliation to mankind and the world at large. In another place he cautions that the church must not underestimate the importance of human example, which has its origin in the humanity of Jesus and is so important in the teaching of Paul, because concrete examples and not concepts give the church's word emphasis and power.

Today we are literally flooded with words. Even in the church words abound. Yet we are rarely moved by them. Overabundance is undoubtedly part of the problem, but the trouble lies deeper than quantity. The real problem is loss of meaning, loss of power, and loss of authenticity. The whole question of man's language and its ability to express meaning—the hermeneutical question—has been raised in a decisive way, and for the church it has become acute with respect to the translation of the meaning of the biblical language into the language of the twentieth century. Many consider this an altogether academic problem, but not Bonhoeffer. For him it was not merely the question of finding the proper language, although obviously it is important when one wants to express himself nonreligiously, that is, without making religion the precondition of faith. The more basic question for Bonhoeffer was whether our lives authenticate or belie our words. Or, to use a common expression: Do we practice what we preach? Do we really mean what we say?

It is our contention that much of the respect paid to Bonhoeffer's words is due to the overall witness of his life. There is always the danger of romanticizing a martyr, of turning him into a religious hero, which must be avoided. Bonhoeffer could not have imagined anything more revolting! Nevertheless, he did leave Germany in protest against Nazi anti-Semitism in 1933. He did leave England and return to the German church struggle in 1935. He did leave America and return to Germany when war

21

was imminent in 1939. He did become involved in the resistance movement against Hitler. And he was hanged to death in a Gestapo concentration camp. These are the more dramatic events, of course, but they give support to our feeling that here was a man whose life witnesses to the integrity and authenticity of his Christian faith. From them we can understand his remark, made at the height of Hitler's persecution of the Jews, that only he who had cried out for the Jews had the right to sing Gregorian chants, or his assertion that action springs not from thought, but from a readiness for responsibility.

Bonhoeffer never bemoaned the fragmentariness of his life, but rejoiced that Christianity plunges man into many dimensions of life simultaneously and allows him to find wholeness in the fragments. Indeed, he compared the fragments to the wealth of themes that are blended together harmoniously in the fugue. They are the melodies of life that provide the counterpoint to the *cantus firmus,* the ground bass, which for the Christian is his faith in God. Bonhoeffer's life was polyphonous because he had a good, clear *cantus firmus.* He could take life in his stride, with all its sorrows and joys, and yet never forget Jeremiah 45, which at least means that it is only by God's grace that we live at all.

The power of Bonhoeffer's words is the power of one who discovered the secret of freedom. He called one of his poems written in prison, ''Stations on the Way to Freedom,'' and the successive stations were discipline, action, suffering, death. He was a man who lived close to

22

God and for his fellow man. If we would be heard, dare we do less?

We now direct our attention briefly to the two writings translated in this volume. Where do they fit into the life of Dietrich Bonhoeffer? What was the occasion for their production, and what is their significance? "Thy Kingdom Come. The Prayer of the Church for God's Kingdom on Earth," stems from the year 1932, when Bonhoeffer was twenty-six years old. At this time he was lecturing at the University of Berlin on "Creation and Fall" and was also intensively engaged in ecumenical activities. At several ecumenical conferences that year he had advocated a doctrine of the "orders of preservation," which he understood to be orders that exist only because they preserve fallen man for Christ, in oppostion to a doctrine of the "orders of creation," which could be used by Nazi-sympathizing theologians to support the party's radical views. This position was the forerunner of the doctrine of the "divine mandates," which he developed in his *Ethics.* Twelve years later, in 1944, "The First Table of the Ten Commandments" was written. Bonhoeffer was now thirty-eight. He had experienced a great deal during those intervening years, and now was writing from a prison cell. It was summer and the same time when he was developing his thoughts about a nonreligious or this-worldly Christianity for a world come of age.

As one might expect, there is a noticeable change in the

style of writing. "Thy Kingdom Come" was prepared as a hard-hitting, passionately earnest lecture to be delivered to the students and faculty of a school in Potsdam-Hermannswerder by the up-and-coming *Privatdozent* of the University of Berlin. The interpretation of the Commandments, on the other hand, represents the calm and mature reflections of a mind tempered by the church struggle and war, resistance and submission, meditation and torture. In both, however, there is the same forthrightness, the same verve, and the same simple wisdom.

Bonhoeffer apparently wrote each of these essays upon request. "Thy Kingdom Come" was his contribution to a series of lectures which Johannes Kühne, the director of the aforementioned school, had arranged to be presented during the last week of the church year, which is known as the "Week of Repentance." On Saturday evening, November 19, 1932, two *Privatdozenten* from the University of Berlin gave addresses; Johannes Schneider, a New Testament scholar, spoke on "The Biblical Message of the Kingdom of God," and Dietrich Bonhoeffer on "Thy Kingdom Come. The Prayer of the Church for God's Kingdom on Earth." The two lectures were published together in 1933 under the title, *The Coming Kingdom,* and appeared as Number 78 in a Furche-Verlag series called "Voices from the Christian Student Movement in Germany."

It is not known who requested Bonhoeffer to write an exposition of the first three Ten Commandments. In one of his illegal letters from prison, dated June 27, 1944, he wrote to his friend Eberhard Bethge, ''At the present time I am writing an exposition of the first three Commandments. I find the first especially difficult. The usual interpretation of idolatry as 'wealth, sensual pleasure, and reputation' seems quite unbiblical to me. That is a bit of moralizing. Idols are to be worshiped, and idolatry presupposes that men still worship something. But today we no longer worship anything, not even idols. In this regard, we are really nihilists.'' On August 3, 1944, he commented to Bethge in an unpublished letter, ''The work on the first three Commandments appears to have been useful, which pleases me.'' Bethge never thought to ask for whom he was writing it, but a copy of the work, written on very poor paper, was saved by Bonhoeffer's fiancée, Maria von Wedemeyer.

Bonhoeffer called his exposition ''The First Table of the Ten Commandments'' (the German is actually ''The First Table of the Ten Words,'' but we thought it better to use the traditional terminology), and it may be helpful to some readers to know what is meant by the ''two tables'' of the Law. The reference is to the two stone tables or tablets on which the Ten Commandments are said to have been inscribed. But more important for our purpose, the first table is customarily thought to have contained those commandments more directly concerned with man's relation to God and the second with relations between man and his neighbor.

But now to Bonhoeffer himself! We leave it to the reader to compare the two writings, to evaluate their contribution to his understanding of the concerns of Christian faith, and to decide for himself whether or not there is anything here akin to "nonreligious interpretation."

JOHN D. GODSEY

Drew University
Madison, New Jersey
July, 1964

THY KINGDOM COME

THE PRAYER OF THE CHURCH
FOR GOD'S KINGDOM
ON EARTH

1932

We are otherworldly, or we are secular—but in either case this means we no longer believe in God's kingdom. We are hostile to the earth because we want to be better than the earth, or we are hostile to God because he deprives us of the earth, our mother; we seek refuge from the power of the earth, or we plant ourselves stubbornly and firmly upon it—but in either case we are not the wanderers who love the earth that bears them. Wanderers who love the earth aright do so only because it is on this earth that they make their approach to that alien land which they love above all else, except for which they would not be wandering at all. Only wanderers of this kind, who love both earth and God at the same time, can believe in the kingdom of God.

We are otherworldly—ever since we hit upon the devious trick of being religious, yes even "Christian," at the expense of the earth. Otherworldliness affords a splendid environment in which to live. Whenever life begins to become oppressive and troublesome a person just leaps into the air with a bold kick and soars relieved and unencumbered into so-called eternal fields. He leaps over the present. He disdains the earth; he is better than it. After all, besides the temporal defeats he still has his eternal victories, and they are so easily achieved. Otherworldliness also makes it easy to preach and to speak words of comfort. An otherworldly church can be certain that it will in no time win over all the weaklings, all who are only too glad to be deceived and deluded, all utopianists, all disloyal sons of the earth. When an explosion seems imminent, who would not be so human as to quickly mount the chariot that comes down from the skies with the promise of taking him to a better world beyond? What church would be so merciless, so inhuman, as not to deal compassionately with this weakness of suffering men—and thereby save souls for the kingdom of heaven? Man is weak; he cannot bear having the earth so near, the earth that bears him. He cannot stand it, because the earth is stronger than he and because he wants to be better than the evil earth. So he extricates himself from it; he refuses to take it seriously. Who could blame him for that—who but the have-nots in their envy? Man is weak, that's just the way he is; and this weakling man is open to the religion of otherworldliness. Should it be denied him? Should the weakling remain without help? Would that be in the spirit of Jesus Christ? No, the weak man should receive help. He does in fact receive help, from Christ. However, Christ does not will or intend this weakness; instead, he makes man strong. He does not lead man in a religious flight from this world to other worlds beyond; rather, he gives him back to the earth as its loyal son.

Be not otherworldly, but be strong!

Or we are children of the world. Whoever feels that what has been said thus far does not apply to him at all

29

had better watch out that what is now about to be said does not strike painfully home. We have fallen into secularism, and by secularism I mean pious, Christian secularism. Not the godlessness of atheism or cultural Bolshevism, but the Christian renunciation of God as the Lord of the earth. In this renunciation it becomes evident that we are indeed bound to the earth. We have to struggle with the earth to come to terms with it. There is no other way. Power stands against power. World stands against church, worldliness against religion. How could it be otherwise than that religion and church are forced into this controversy, into this struggle? Moreover, faith is compelled to harden into religious habit and into morality, and the church must become an organ for effecting religious and moral reconstruction. So faith spruces up its weapons because the powers of the earth compel it to do so. After all, we are supposed to represent God's cause. We have to build for ourselves a strong fortress in which we dwell safe and secure with God. We will build the kingdom.

This joyous secularism also affords a splendid environment in which to live. Man—even religious man—likes a good fight; he likes to put his strength to the test. Who would begrudge him this gift of nature—who but the have-nots in their envy? This pious secularism also makes it possible to preach and to say nice things. The church may be certain, if only it makes a somewhat more spirited effort in this direction, that it soon will have on its side in this happy war all the brave, the resolute, the well-in-tentioned, all the overly loyal sons of the earth. What upright man would not gladly represent the cause of God in this wicked world and do as the ancient Egyptians are said to have done? They carried the images of their gods against the enemy—in order to hide behind them! Only now man wants to hide not just from the enemy, the world, but from God himself, from that God who destroys whoever would front for him on earth. It is not God's will that any man, on the sheer strength of his own superabundant power, should take over for God on earth, like the strong take care of the helpless. On the contrary, God manages his own cause; and out of his own free grace he accepts man, or does not accept him. God himself intends to be Lord on earth, and he regards all man's exuberant zeal on His behalf as a real disservice. Herein lies our Christian secularism, that in our very desire to see that God gets everything that is his due in the world we actually evade God himself, and so love the earth for its own sake, for the sake of this struggle. But we do not thereby really elude God. He always brings us back under his own lordship.

Become weak in the world and let God be the Lord!

Now otherworldliness and secularism are only two sides of the same thing, namely, disbelief in God's kingdom. They disbelieve who would flee the world to reach it, seeking it in a place removed from all their troubles; and they also disbelieve who suppose that they are to erect it themselves as a kingdom of this world. Whoever evades the earth does not find God. He finds only another world: his own, better, more beautiful, more peaceful world. He finds a world beyond, to be sure, but one that is not God's world, that world which is dawning in this world. Whoever evades the earth in order to find God, finds only himself. Whoever evades God in order to find the earth does not find God's earth; he finds only the jolly battleground of a war which he himself incites, a war between the good people and the bad, the pious and the blasphemers—in short, he finds himself. Whoever loves God, on the other hand, loves him as Lord of the earth as it is; and whoever loves the earth loves it as God's earth. Whoever loves God's kingdom, loves it wholly as God's kingdom, but he also loves it wholly as God's kingdom on earth. And he does so because the King of the kingdom is the Creator and Preserver of the earth, who has blessed the earth, and who created us out of it.

But—God has cursed the blessed earth; we live on the cursed ground that bears thorns and thistles. But—it is to this cursed earth that Christ has come; the flesh Christ bore was taken from this ground; on this ground the Tree of the curse has stood. And it is this second "but" that establishes the kingdom of Christ as God's kingdom here on the cursed ground. Thus the kingdom of Christ is a kingdom that, coming from above, is sunk down into the cursed ground. It is here present, but as the hidden treasure in the cursed ground. We pass it by without even knowing it, but the fact that it goes unseen becomes a judgment upon ourselves: "You have seen only the ground, its thistles and thorns, maybe even its seed and its grain, but you have not found the hidden treasure in the cursed ground." Indeed, it is this hiddenness which really constitutes the curse that weighs upon the ground of the earth: not that it bears thistles and thorns, but that it conceals God's countenance, so that even the deepest furrows of the earth do not unveil for us the hidden God.

If we are to pray for the coming of the kingdom, we can do so only as those who are wholly on earth. No one can pray for the kingdom who tears himself away from his own troubles and the troubles of others, who in the detachment and seclusion of his meditative moments is concerned only for his own salvation. There may be times when the church can endure even that, but this is not one of them. The hour in which the church today prays for the kingdom is one that forces the church, for good or ill, to identify itself completely with the children of the earth and of the world. It binds the church by oaths of fealty to the earth, to misery, to hunger, to death. It makes the church stand in full solidarity with evil and with the guilt of the brother. The hour in which we today pray for God's kingdom is the hour of utmost togetherness with the world, a time of clenched teeth and trembling fist. It is no time for solitary whispering, "O that I may be saved,'' but for joining in the common silence that cries aloud, "O that this world, which has forged us into a unity in the crucible of grief and pain, may pass away, and thy kingdom come to us.'' It is the eternal right of Prometheus to love the earth, the earth which is "the mother of all'' (Ecclus. 40:1); it is this right which allows him to draw near the kingdom of God, in a way that the coward fleeing to worlds beyond cannot.

No one can pray for the kingdom either who thinks up a kingdom for himself in terms of boldly conceived Utopias, of dreams and hopes, who lives for his own world-view and knows a thousand programs and prescriptions by which he would like to cure the world. If we just take an honest look at ourselves sometime when we catch ourselves thinking such thoughts, we'll be in for a real surprise. None of us knows what it is he really wants. The question is a very simple one: Just how do you conceive your kingdom of God on earth? What do you really want men to be like? More moral, more pious, more homogeneous? Should they be less emotional? No longer sick and hungry, or subject to death? Should there no longer be the intelligent and the ignorant, the strong and the weak, the poor and the rich? It is actually astonishing that the moment we honestly try to ask and to answer this question we no longer know which way to turn. We want the one all right, but then—for good reasons—we don't want it either. If we think at all seriously and honestly about it, we must realize that

it is utterly impossible for us to come up with any kind
of a Utopian scheme for a kingdom of God on earth. The
possibility of thinking in universal terms, of achieving a
comprehensive view of things, is simply closed to us. All
our hopes of turning the cursed ground into the blessed
ground, and thus regaining it, are doomed by the fact that
it is God himself who cursed the ground, and is alone
able to take back what he said and bless the earth again.
We must be aroused from the intoxication with which
the poison of the cursed earth has drugged us; we must
be sobered up. The earth wants us to take it seriously. It
will not let us escape, either into the salvation of otherworldly piety or into the Utopia of a this-worldly secularism. Instead, it comes right out and shows us how it is
enslaved in finitude. The earth's enslavement though is
our enslavement as well; with it we too are subjugated.

Death, loneliness, and desire—these are the three
powers that enslave the earth. Better, these are the one
power, the adversary or evil one, who will not surrender
the rights he has gained over the fallen creation. Better
yet, these are the power of the curse that came forth from
the mouth of the Creator. And this is why with our
Utopias we do not get beyond our own death, loneliness,
and desire; they all belong inextricably to the cursed earth.
But in fact we are not supposed to get beyond them at
all. On the contrary, the kingdom comes to us, comes
into our death, into our loneliness, into our desire. It
comes precisely there where the church perseveres in soli-

darity with the world and expects the kingdom solely from God.

"Thy kingdom come"—this is not the prayer of the pious individual who wants to flee from the world, nor is it the prayer of the fanatical utopianist who stubbornly insists on reforming the world. Rather, this prayer is prayed solely by the congregation of the children of the earth, who refuse to separate themselves from the world and who have no special proposals to offer for its improvement. The people of this community also do not consider themselves superior to the world, but persevere together in the midst of the world, in its depths, in its trivialities and bondages. They persevere because in this kind of existence they now demonstrate their loyalty in their own curious way, and they steadfastly keep their eyes on that strange place in this world where they perceive in utter amazement God's breaking through the curse, his unfathomable "Yes!" to the world. Here at the very center of this dying, disrupted, and desirous world something becomes evident to those who can believe— believe in the resurrection of Jesus Christ. Here the absolute miracle has occurred. Here the law of death is shattered. Here the kingdom of God itself comes to us on earth, comes into our world. Here God binds himself to the world and gives the blessing that abolishes the curse. It is actually this occurrence alone that kindles the prayer for the kingdom. It is just in this occurrence that the old earth is affirmed and that God is hailed as Lord of the earth. Again, it is this occurrence that overcomes, breaks through, and destroys the cursed earth, and promises the new earth. God's kingdom is the kingdom of the resurrection on earth.

We struggle against this kingdom with our two-faced infidelity. We place limits for God by declaring in feigned humility that God cannot come to us because he is too great. His kingdom is not meant for this earth. God and his kingdom are found only in an eternal beyond. But what humility could presume to determine the limits of God's action—the limits of him who died and rose again? This humility is nothing other than the poorly concealed pride of those who themselves pretend to know what God's kingdom is and who now, in just as poorly concealed zeal, want to perform the miracle themselves. They themselves want to build the kingdom of God, and they perceive the coming of this kingdom in the strengthening of the church, the Christianizing of culture, politics, and education, and a renewing of Christian practices. In this way they simply fall again under the curse of the earth, in which the kingdom of God is hidden like a treasure. Who could so completely deceive themselves that they do not see that it is God himself, and God alone, who effects this breakthrough, this miracle, namely, the kingdom of the resurrection?

It is not a matter of what God could do and what we could do, but rather of what God has done for us, and wants to do again and again, that provides the basis for

37

our prayer for the coming of the kingdom. The kingdom of God is meant for the earth; it comes to this earth that stands under the curse. It breaks through the law of death, of loneliness, and of desire in the world, and it is entirely God's kingdom, his action, his word, his rising from the dead. It really is the miracle, God's miracle of breaking through death to life, and it is this miracle that supports our faith and our prayer for the kingdom. Why should we be ashamed that we have a God who performs miracles, who creates life and conquers death? A ''god'' who can perform no miracle—that would be a description of ourselves! If God is really God, then he himself, as well as his kingdom, is miraculous—indeed, the absolute miracle! Why are we so anxious, so cautious, so cowardly? God will shame us all when one day he lets us see things that are a thousand times more miraculous than anything till now. We will be ashamed before him, the miraculous God. Thus we look upon his miraculous action and pray, ''Thy kingdom come to us.''

The petition for the kingdom is not the begging of the anxious soul for its own salvation. It is not Christian trimmings to be used by those who would reform the world. It is rather the petition of the suffering and battling congregation in the world on behalf of the human race, asking that God fully manifest his glory in it. Our question today is not about God and the individual, but God and mankind. Our prayer today is not that God should come to dwell in our souls, but that God should create his kingdom in our midst. But how does God's kingdom come to us? The answer is that it comes in exactly the same way that God himself comes, namely, in breaking through the law of death, in the resurrection, in the miracle; and yet, at the same time, in the "Yes" to the earth, in his entering into its orders, its communities, its history. Both ways belong inextricably together, because only where the earth is fully affirmed can its curse be seriously broken through and destroyed, and only the fact that the earth's curse is broken permits the earth to be taken with real seriousness. In other words, God manages the earth in such a way that he breaks through its law of death. Thus God is always both the one who binds himself to the earth and the one who breaks its curse.

The earth to which God binds himself is the earth he preserves, the earth that is fallen, lost, and cursed. He binds himself to it as he does to his work. But where God is, there also is his kingdom. God always comes with his kingdom. His kingdom must go the same way he goes. It comes with him to the earth, and it is present among us in no other way than in a twofold form: first, as the final kingdom of the miraculous resurrection that breaks through, negates, overcomes, and destroys all kingdoms of the earth, all the kingdoms built by man, which are subject to the curse of death; and, second, and simultaneously, as the kingdom of order that affirms and preserves the earth with its laws, communities, and history. Miracle and order—these are the two forms in which the kingdom of God appears on earth. The kingdom is always divided in this way: miracle as breaking through all order, and order as preservation in preparation for the miracle; but also, miracle completely veiled in the world of orders, and order enduring completely by virtue of its being limited by miracle. The form in which the kingdom of God attests itself as miracle we call the church; the form in which it attests itself as order we call the state.

The kingdom of God exists in our world exclusively in the duality of church and state. Each is necessarily related to the other; neither exists for itself. Every attempt of one to take control of the other disregards this relationship of the kingdom of God on earth. Every prayer for the coming of the kingdom to us that does not have in mind both church and state is either otherworldliness or secularism. It is, in any case, disbelief in the kingdom of God.

The kingdom of God assumes form in the church insofar as the church bears witness to the miracle of God. The function of the church is to witness to the resurrection of Christ from the dead, to the end of the law of death of this world that stands under the curse, and to the power of God in the new creation. The kingdom of God assumes form in the state insofar as the state acknowledges and maintains the order of the preservation of life, and insofar as it holds itself responsible for protecting this world from flying to pieces and for exercising its authority here in preventing the destruction of life. Its function is not to create new life, but to preserve the life that is given.

Therefore, the power of death, of which we spoke, is destroyed in the church by the authoritative witness to the miracle of the resurrection, whereas in the state it is restrained by the order of the preservation of life. With its complete authority, with which it knows itself solely responsible for the order of life, the state points to the church's witness to the breaking up of the law of death in the world of the resurrection; and with its witness to the resurrection, the church points to the preserving, ordering action of the state in the preserved world of the curse. Thus they both witness to the kingdom of God, which is entirely God's kingdom and wholly a kingdom for us.

The kingdom of God assumes form in the church insofar as here the loneliness of man is overcome through the miracle of confession and forgiveness. This is because in the church, which is the communion of saints created by the resurrection, one person can and should bear the guilt of another, and for this reason the last shackle of loneliness, hatred of others, is removed, and community is established and created anew. It is through the miracle of confession, which is beyond all our understanding, that all hitherto existing community is shown to have been an illusion and is abolished, destroyed, and broken asunder, and that here and now the new congregation of the resurrection world is created.

The kingdom of God assumes form in the state insofar as here the orders of existing communities are maintained with authority and responsibility. Lest mankind fall apart through the desires of individuals who want simply to go their own way, the state takes the responsibility in a world under the curse for the preservation of the orders of communities, such as marriage, family, and nation. Not the creation of new communities, but the preservation of communities as given is the function of the state.

In the church the power of loneliness is destroyed in the confession-occurrence; in the state it is restrained through the preservation of community order. And, again, in its limited action the state points to the final miracle of God in the resurrection, just as in its authoritative witness to God's breaking through to the world, the church points to the maintenance of order in the world under the curse.

The kingdom of God assumes form in the church insofar as the power of desire is transfigured through the testimony of God's miracle. The desire of man, who is wholly turned in upon himself, is condemned, nullified, and destroyed in the proclamation of the cross and the resurrection of Jesus Christ. At the crucified body of Christ our desire is judged. Yet, at the same time, it is transfigured and created anew in the resurrection world, where it becomes the desire of one person for another, the desire for God and the brother, and thus for love, for peace, joy, and blessedness.

The kingdom of God assumes form in the state insofar as here man's desire is held in check with authority and responsibility and is kept within the order; that is, insofar as each man is protected and saved from the desire of another. Yet the desire is not obliterated but merely restrained, so that it may prove its value and bear fruit in the service of the community of the fallen world. Love is also present here—but always marked by the possibility of hate; joy, too, is to be found here—but never without the bitter consciousness of its transiency; and even blessedness—but always on the edge of despair.

In the church the power of desire is overcome and transfigured, whereas in the state it is regulated and held in check. Here also the limited action of the state points to the authoritative testimony of the church, just as the church points to the order of the state, which in this world under the curse carries out its function.

The church limits the state, just as the state limits the church, and each must remain conscious of this mutual limitation. Furthermore, each must bear the tension of coexistence, which in this world must never be a coalescence. Only thus do both together, never one alone, point to the kingdom of God, which here is attested in such a wonderful twofold form.

This consideration does not remain theoretical, but really gets serious at the point where we who are between church and state speak of the people. Because the people are called to the kingdom of God, they have a place in both state and church. As a result, the people, indeed we ourselves, now provide the setting for the encounter between church and state. We ourselves become those who are called, on the one hand, to take the limits seriously, and, on the other, where the limits really clash and produce sparks, to perceive the living heart of the kingdom of God itself. When we pray, "Thy kingdom come," then we pray for the church, that it may bear witness to the miracle of God's resurrection, and for the state, that with its authority it may defend the orders of the preserved world of the curse. That the church will execute its function solely in relation to the miracle and the state solely in relation to the order, and that between church and state the people of God, Christendom, will live obediently—this is the prayer for the kingdom of God on earth, for the kingdom of Christ.

The kingdom of Christ is God's kingdom, but God's kingdom in the form appointed for us. It does not appear as one, visible, powerful empire, nor yet as the "new" kingdom of the world; on the contrary, it manifests itself as the kingdom of the other world that has entered completely into the discord and contradiction of this world. It appears as the powerless, defenseless gospel of the resurrection, of the miracle; and, at the very same time, as the state that possesses authority and power and maintains order. The kingdom of Christ becomes a reality only when these two are genuinely related to each other and yet mutually limit one another.

What has been said so far may sound sober, and it is

supposed to; only in this way are we called to obedience, namely, when it is understood as obedience to God in the church and in the state. The kingdom of God is not to be found in some other world beyond, but in the midst of this world. Our obedience is demanded in terms of its contradictory appearance, and, then, through our obedience, the miracle, like lightning, is allowed to flash up again and again from that perfect, blessed new world of the final promise. God wants us to honor him on earth; he wants us to honor him in our fellow man—and nowhere else. He sinks his kingdom down into the cursed ground. Let us open our eyes, become sober, and obey him here. "Come, O blessed of my Father, inherit the kingdom!" This the Lord will say to no other than the one to whom he says, "I was hungry and you gave me food, I was thirsty and you gave me drink. . . . As you did it to one of the least of these my brethren, you did it to me" (Matt. 25:34, 35, 40).

Because the kingdom of God is to exist eternally, God will create a new heaven and a new earth. But it will really be a new earth. Even then there will be a kingdom of God on earth, on the new earth of promise, on the old earth of the creation. The promise consists in this: that one day we shall behold the world of the resurrection, that world which is now comprehended in the word of the church and to which the state points. We shall not remain in discord, but God will be all in all. Christ will lay his kingdom at his feet, and the kingdom of the consummation will be at hand. This is the kingdom in which there will be no more tears, no more sorrow, no more crying, no more death; it is the kingdom of life, of fellowship, and of glorification. Then church and state will exist no longer. Rather, they will give back their offices to him from whom they originally received them, and he alone will be the Lord as the Creator, the crucified and resurrected One, and the Spirit who pervades his holy congregation.

"Thy kingdom come." Thus we pray also for that final kingdom out of the certainty that his kingdom has already dawned in our midst. It comes even without our prayer, says Luther, but we ask in this prayer that it may come also to us, that we may not be left outside.

In the Old Testament we are told the strange story of Jacob, who has fled from his homeland, from the promised land of God, and has lived many years in a foreign land in a state of enmity with his brother. Now he can no longer bear to stay; he wants to return home to the land of promise, to go back to his brother. He is on his way; it is the last night before he is to set foot again on the promised land. Only a small river still separates him from his homeland. As he prepares to cross it, he is stopped. A stranger wrestles with him in the dark. It seems that Jacob will not be allowed to return to his homeland, but will be overpowered at the door to the promised land and put to death. But unprecedented powers come upon Jacob, and he stands up to his opponent and clasps his arms around him. He does not let loose until he hears him say, "Let me go, for the day is breaking." Then Jacob summons his utmost strength; he refuses to release him. "I will not let you go, unless you bless me." It seems to him as if the end has come; his strong opponent handles him so roughly. Yet at this moment he hears the blessing, and the stranger is no longer there. Then the sun rises upon Jacob, and he proceeds into the promised land, limping because his thigh has been put out of joint. The way is clear; the dark door to the land of promise has been broken open. The blessing has come from out of the curse, and now the sun shines upon him.

That the way of all of us into the land of promise leads through the night; that we also only enter it as those who are perhaps curiously scarred from the struggle with God, the struggle for his kingdom and his grace; and that we enter the land of God and of our brother as limping warriors—all these things we Christians have in common with Jacob. And we know too that the sun is destined also for us, and this knowledge allows us to bear with patience the time of wandering and waiting and believing that is imposed upon us. But beyond Jacob, we know something else. We know that it is not we who must go; we know that He comes to us. Our consolation on this eve of the final Sunday in the church year is our knowledge that Advent and Christmas follow. That is why we pray, "Thy kingdom come to us."

THE FIRST TABLE OF THE
TEN COMMANDMENTS
1944

In the midst of thunder, lightning, thick clouds, mountain quaking, and loud trumpet blasts, God makes known the Ten Commandments to his servant Moses on Mount Sinai. They are not the result of long reflection upon human life and its orders by wise and experienced men; rather, they are God's word of revelation, amidst which the earth quakes and the elements are in a tumult. The Ten Commandments enter into the world not as universal worldly wisdom, which is available to any thinking man, but as a holy event which even the people of God may not approach, under threat of death. They come as God's revelation in the isolation of a smoking volcano peak. Moses does not give them; rather, God gives them. Moses does not write them; rather, God himself writes them on stone tables with his finger, as the Bible emphasizes time and again. "He added no more" (Deut. 5:22), which means, God himself wrote only these words; they contain the whole will of God. The superiority of the Ten Commandments to all other words of God is most clearly manifested by the safekeeping of the two tables in the ark of the covenant in the holy of holies, the most sacred part of the sanctuary. The Ten Commandments belong in the sanctuary. They must be sought there, at the place of God's gracious presence in the world, and from there they go forth again and again into the world (Isa. 2:3).

In all ages men have thought about the fundamental orders of life, and it is an exceedingly noteworthy fact that the results of almost all such reflections agree extensively with each other and with the Ten Comandments. It is always the case that when men's living conditions are thrown into disorder by outer or inner commotions and upheavals, those men who are able to retain lucidity and sobriety of thought and judgment realize that no human communal life is possible without a fear of God and a respect for parents, and without the protection of life, marriage, property, and reputation—regardless of how these principles may be formulated. In order to recognize these laws of life, a man does not need to be a Christian, but needs only to follow his experience and sound reason. The Christian rejoices that he holds so many important things in common with other men. He is ready to work and to struggle alongside these men, where it is a matter of the realization of common goals. It does not surprise him that men in every age have come to understandings of life that agree extensively with the Ten Commandments, because the Giver of the Commandments is indeed the Creator and Preserver of life. Still, the Christian never forgets the decisive difference that exists between these laws of life and the Commandments of God. In the former, reason speaks; in the latter, God. Human reason predicts that life itself will take revenge on the transgressor of the laws of life, in that after an initial ostensible success, it leads him to shipwreck and misfortune. But God speaks not of life with its successes and failures; rather, he speaks of himself. God's first word in the Ten Commandments is "I." It is with this "I" that man must reckon, not with some general law; not with a "one should do this or that," but rather with the living

God. In each word of the Ten Commandments God speaks basically of himself, and that is the principal thing in them. It is for this reason they are God's revelation. In the Ten Commandments we obey not a law but God, and when we transgress them, we run aground not on a law but on God himself. Not only confusion and failure come upon the transgressor, but God's wrath. It is not only unwise but it is sin to disregard the Commandment of God, and the wages of sin is death. Hence the New Testament calls the Ten Commandments "living words" (Acts 7:38).

Instead of "Ten Commandments," perhaps we would do better to follow the Bible in saying the "Ten Words" of God (Deut. 4:13). Then we would not confuse them so easily with human laws, and also we would not set aside so lightly the first words, "I am the Lord your God," as a mere preface that really does not belong to and go with the Commandments at all. In truth, however, just these initial words are the most important of all; indeed, they are the key to the Ten Commandments. They show us wherein God's Commandment differs eternally from human laws. In the Ten Commandments God speaks just as much of his grace as he does of his Commandment. They are not something we can separate from God, as it were, and then label "God's will." On the contrary, in them the whole, living God reveals himself to be who he is. This is the basic point.

The Ten Commandments, as we know them, are an

abridgement of the biblical text. Wherein lies the warrant for such a deviation from the Bible at so decisive a place? The universal Christian church hears the Ten Commandments in a different way than the people of Israel. That which belongs to Israel's situation as a political people is not obligatory for the Christian church, which is a spiritual people among all peoples. Thus, in the freedom of faith in the God of the Commandments, the church has ventured to let a spiritually interpreted version take the place of a literal version of the biblical text.

"I am the Lord your God." When God says "I," then revelation has occurred. God could also let the world take its course and keep silent. Why should God need to speak of himself? When God says "I," it is grace. When God says "I," then with that he says absolutely everything, from beginning to end. When God says "I," it means, "Prepare to meet your God!" (Amos 4:12).

"I am the Lord." Not *a* Lord, but *the* Lord! Therewith God claims dominion for himself alone. All right to command and all obedience belong solely to him. Since God attests himself as Lord, he delivers us from all enslavement to man. There is, and we have, only one Master, and "no one can serve two masters." We serve solely God and no man. Even when we carry out the orders of earthly masters, in truth we serve only God. It is a great error of many Christians to suppose that for the time of our earthly life God has subjugated us to many masters besides himself and to suppose that our life stands in a constant conflict between the orders of these earthly masters and his Commandment. We have only one Lord to whom we owe obedience. Moreover, his orders are clear and do not plunge us into conflict. To be sure, God has given parents and governments on earth the right and power to give us commands, but all earthly dominion is grounded exclusively in the dominion of God. It has its authority and dignity in God's sovereignty; otherwise it is usurpation and has no claim to obedience. Because we obey only the Commandment of God, we also obey our parents and the government. Our obedience to God commits us to obedience to parents and government. However, not every obedience to parents and government is necessarily obedience to God. We really obey solely God, never man. "Whatever your task, work heartily, as serving the Lord and not men" (Col. 3:23). "You were bought with a price; do not become slaves of men" (I Cor. 7:23). Obedience to God alone is the foundation of our freedom.

God the Lord, however, has not only the sole right to command, but also the sole power to enforce his Commandment. All means stand at his disposal. Whoever sets himself up as Lord alongside of him must fall. Whoever despises his Commandment must die. But he who serves him alone and relies on him, the Lord defends and supports and provides a reward, both in time and in eternity.

"Your God." God speaks to his chosen people, to the congregation that hears him in faith. For it the Lord, the inaccessibly distant and powerful One, is at the same time the near, present, and merciful One. "For what great nation is there that has a god so near to it as the Lord our God is to us, whenever we call upon him?" (Deut. 4:7). We are not concerned here with a foreigner or a tyrant or some blind fate that imposes upon us intolerable burdens, under which we would be crushed, but rather with God the Lord, who has elected, created, and loved us, who knows us, who wants to be near us, for us, and with us. He gives us the Commandments in order that we can be and remain near him, for him, and with him. He commits himself to us, in that he, as Lord and Helper, makes known to us his Commandment. "He has not dealt thus with any other nation" (Ps. 147:20). God is so great that to him the smallest is not too small; he is so very much the Lord that he steps to our side as our Helper. When God is with us, then his Commandments are not difficult. Then his law is our consolation (Ps. 119:92), his yoke easy, his burden light. "I will run in the way of thy commandments when thou consolest my heart!" (Ps. 119:32). In the ark of the covenant, which is the throne of the gracious presence of God, lie both tables, enclosed, surrounded, and covered by the grace of God. Whoever wishes to speak of the Ten Commandments must seek them in the ark of the covenant, and so must, at the same time, speak of God's grace. Whoever wishes

55

to proclaim the Ten Commandments must, at the same time, proclaim God's boundless grace.

THE FIRST COMMANDMENT

"You shall have no other gods beside me." The "You shall not," which now follows ten times in succession, is nothing other than the exposition of the preceding self-attestation of God. What it means for our life that God is the Lord and our God is told us in ten short sentences. The connection becomes most obvious when we insert a "therefore" before each of these sentences. "I am the Lord your God; *therefore* you shall not . . . ." It is a sign of God's goodness that by such prohibitions he wants to protect us from errors and transgressions and to indicate the bounds within which we can live in communion with him.

"You shall not have other gods beside me." This is by no means self-evident. Peoples of advanced cultures have always known a heaven of the gods, and it belonged to the greatness and dignity of a god that he did not jealously contest the place of another in the pious hearts of men. The human virtue of magnanimity and tolerance was also ascribed to the gods. But God tolerates no other god beside him; he wants to be the only God. He wants to do and to be everything for man; for this reason he also wants to be the only one worshiped by him. Beside him, nothing has a place; under him, the entire creation. God wants alone to be God, because he alone is God.

Here the concern is not that we could worship other gods in place of God, but that we could suppose that we can place anything at all *beside* God. There are Christians who say that beside their faith in God, which they would never let go of, the world, the state, work, family, science, art, and nature also have their right. God says that nothing whatsoever has any right beside him, only under him. Whatever we place beside God is an idol.

It is often said that our idols are money, sensuality, reputation, other men, and we ourselves. It would be still more appropriate if we would designate as our idols our display of strength, our power, our success. But in their weakness men actually have always fixed their hearts on all these things, and none of what has been mentioned is actually meant by the First Commandment when it speaks of ''other gods.'' For us the world has lost its gods; we no longer worship anything. We have experienced too clearly the frailty and invalidity of all things, of all men, and of ourselves for us still to be able to deify them. We have lost too much confidence in the whole of existence for us still to be capable of having and worshiping gods. If we still have an idol, perhaps it is nothingness, obliteration, meaninglessness. So the First Commandment calls us to the sole, true God, to the omnipotent, righteous, and merciful One, who saves us from falling into nothingness and sustains us in his congregation.

There have been times when secular governments have inflicted severe punishment on those who denied God or committed idolatry. Even when this happened with the intention of protecting the community from being misled and from confusion, God was still not served by it, because, first of all, God wants to be freely worshiped. Furthermore, according to God's plan the powers of seduction must serve to confirm and strengthen the faithful. And, finally, our open denial of God is still more full of promise than a hypocritical confession extorted by force. The secular government should grant external protection to faith in the God of the Ten Commandments; but controversy with unbelief should be left solely to the power of the Word of God.

It is not always easy to determine the point at which an action that is ordered by the state turns into idolatry. The early Christians refused to contribute a single grain of incense as a sacrifice to the Roman emperor cult, and on that account they suffered martyrs' deaths. The three men in the third chapter of the Book of Daniel refused to obey the king's order to fall down and worship the golden image, which represented the authority of the king and of his kingdom. On the other hand, the prophet Elisha expressly permitted the Syrian army commander, Naaman, to bow down in the pagan temple when he had to accompany his king (II Kings 5:18). The majority of Christians in Japan have recently declared that participation in the state emperor cult is permitted. In all decisions of this nature the following points are to be considered: (1) When participation in such acts of the state is demanded, is it clearly a matter of the worship of other gods? If it is, then refusal is the clear obligation of Christians. (2) If there is doubt about whether it is a religious or a political act, then the decision will depend on whether by a Christian's participation in it, the church of Christ and the world are offended, that is, if by participation at least the appearance of a denial of Jesus Christ is given. If this is not the case according to the common judgment of the Christians, then nothing stands in the way of participation. But if it is the case, then here also participation will have to be refused.

The Lutheran church has contracted the second biblical commandment, that of the prohibition of images, into the first. What is prohibited to the church is not the figurative representation of God. God himself assumed human form in Jesus Christ and allowed himself to be seen by human eyes. What is prohibited is only the worship or veneration of images, as if they were imbued with divine power. Under the same prohibition falls the superstitious veneration of amulets, guardian devices, and similar things, as though they possessed a special power to guard against misfortune.

"Hear, O Israel: The Lord our God is our Lord; and you shall love the Lord your God with all your heart, and with all your soul, and with all your might" (Deut. 6:4). To this our God we pray with complete confidence, as Jesus Christ has taught us, "Our Father, who art in heaven."

59

THE SECOND COMMANDMENT

"You shall not take the name of the Lord your God in vain; for the Lord will not hold him guiltless who takes his name in vain."

"God" for us is not a general concept with which we designate the highest, holiest, and mightiest that can be conceived. On the contrary, "God" is a name. When pagans say "God," they mean something completely different from what we mean when we, to whom God himself has spoken, say "God." For us, God is our God, the Lord, the Living One. "God" is a name, and this name is the greatest sanctuary that we possess, because we have in it not at all something that we have conceived, but God himself in his whole essence, in his revelation. God in inconceivable grace has given himself to be known by us, and it is solely for this reason that we may say "God." When we say "God," it is as if we were hearing, as it were, God himself speaking to us, calling us, comforting and commanding us. We are conscious of his dealing with us—creating, judging, and admonishing. "We give thanks to thee, O God, that thy name is so near" (Ps. 75:1). "The name of the Lord is a strong tower; the righteous man runs into it and is safe" (Prov. 18:10). The word "God" is nothing at all; the name "God" is everything.

Today men frequently have a feeling that God is not only a word, but a name. For this reason they often avoid saying "God" and speak instead of "divinity," "fate," "providence," "nature," or "the Almighty." For them, "God" already sounds almost like a confession. They do not want that. They want the word, but not the name, because the name obligates.

The Second Commandment calls us to hallow the name of God. Only those who know the name of God can actually transgress the Second Commandment. The word "God" is no more and no less than other human words, and those who misuse it dishonor only themselves and their own thoughts. But whoever knows the name of God and misuses it dishonors and violates the sanctity of God.

The Second Commandment does not speak of the blaspheming of the name of God, but of its misuse, just as the First Commandment did not speak of the denial of God, but of placing other gods beside God. The danger for believers is not blasphemy, but misuse.

We who know the name of God misuse it when we utter it as if it were only a word, as if God himself did not always speak to us in this name. There is a misuse of the name of God with evil intentions and with good intentions. Among Christians, to be sure, the misuse with evil intentions is difficult to envisage, and yet it happens. When we call upon and appeal to the name of God in order consciously to permit a godless, evil cause to appear before the world as pious and good, when we entreat God for his blessing on an evil matter, when we name the name of God in a connection that brings shame upon it—then we misuse it for evil. We know very well that God

61

himself would always speak only against this cause for which we claim him, but because his name is a power, even before the world, we appeal to it.

The misuse of the name of God with good intentions is more dangerous, because it is more difficult to recognize. It occurs when we Christians constantly utter the name of God so self-evidently, so glibly, and so intimately that we detract from the sanctity and the miracle of his revelation. It is misuse when, for every human question and affliction, we are on hand precipitately with the word "God" or with a Bible quotation, as if it were the most self-evident thing in the world that God answers all human questions and is always prepared to help in every difficulty. It is misuse when we make God into a stopgap for our embarrassments. It is misuse when we want to put a stop to genuinely scientific or artistic endeavors simply with the word "God." It is misuse when we throw what is sacred to the dogs. It is misuse when we speak about God without being aware of his living presence in his name. It is misuse when we talk of God as if we had him at all times at our disposal, and as if we had sat in his council. In all these ways we misuse the name of God, because we make it into an empty human word and impotent idle chatter, and in this way we desecrate it more than the blasphemers can desecrate it.

The Israelites met the danger of such misuse of the name of God by the prohibition against pronouncing this name at all. We can only learn from the reverence that is manifest in this regulation. It is certainly better not to pronounce the name of God than to degrade it to a mere human word. Yet we have the sacred commission and the high privilege to bear witness to God before one another and before the world. That happens when we utter the name of God only in such a way that in it the word of the living, present, righteous, and gracious God himself is attested. That can only occur when we daily pray as Jesus Christ has taught us, "Hallowed be thy name!"

The secular governments of the West have from time immemorial ordained punishment for the public blasphemy of God. By this provision they have demonstrated that they are called to protect the belief in God and the worship service from disparagement and abuse. But they never succeeded in suppressing the intellectual movements which, in their rightly or wrongly understood exaggerations, lead to such abuses, and this task can never be theirs. The church is not helped by the violent suppression of intellectual movements. It demands only the freedom of its proclamation and its life, and it trusts the rightly attested name of God to make its own way and to gain respect for itself.

Is it misuse if a person uses the name of God in swearing an oath? As far as the content of the Christian's testimony is concerned, it makes no difference whether he stands under oath or not, or whether he uses the so-called religious or the nonreligious form of oath. His yes is yes, his no is no, regardless of what formula he adds. Among

63

Christians there is no oath, but only yes and no. Solely for the sake of other men and for the sake of the lie that rules in the world, he may make his word—to be sure, not more truthful than it otherwise would be, but yet—more credible, in that he makes use of the form of oath demanded by the state. In such a case it is irrelevant to him whether this form uses the name of God or not. For the Christian the oath signifies only the outward confirmation of what for him is certain anyway, namely, that his word is spoken before God.

THE THIRD COMMANDMENT

"You shall hallow the holiday."

That this Commandment stands on a par with the prohibition of idol worship or even the prohibition of killing, that the transgressor of this Commandment is just as guilty as one who dishonors his parents, or as the thief, or the adulterer, or the slanderer, is difficult for us to conceive. Our usual life consists of days of work in the midst of other men. The holiday appears to us to be a lovely and joyous break in the routine, but that the seriousness of the Commandment of God stands behind it has become foreign to us.

God commands us to keep the holiday. He commands holiday rest and holiday hallowing.

The Decalog contains no commandment to work, but a commandment to rest from work! This is the reverse of what we are accustomed to thinking. In the Third Commandment it is presupposed that it is natural for man to work, but God knows that the work that man does gains such a power over him that he can no longer leave it. Man expects everything from his own action and meanwhile forgets God. For this reason God commands him to rest from his labors. Work does not sustain man; on the contrary, God alone sustains him. Man does not live by work, but solely by God. "Unless the Lord builds the house, those who build it labor in vain. Unless the Lord watches over the city, the watchman stays awake in vain. . . . The Lord gives to his friends while they sleep" (Ps. 127:1, 2). This is the message of the Bible to all who make a religion out of their work. The holiday rest is the visible sign that man lives from the grace of God, and not from works.

Outer and inner rest should rule on the holiday. In our homes all work that is not indispensable for living should cease, and the Decalog expressly includes in this Commandment servants and sojourners, yes, even cattle. We should seek not unplanned diversion, but rest and composure. Because this is not easy, because for us inactivity easily turns into empty idleness, into fatiguing distractions and amusements, resting must be expressly commanded. It requires strength to obey this Commandment.

The holiday rest is the indispensable presupposition of the holiday hallowing. The overtired man, who is degraded to the state of being a machine, needs rest in order that his thinking can again become clear, his feeling purified, and his will reoriented.

The holiday hallowing is the content of the holiday

rest. The hallowing of the holiday takes place through the proclamation of the Word of God in the worship service and through the willing and reverent hearing of this Word. The desecration of the holiday begins with the deterioration of the Christian proclamation. Therefore, it is first of all the church's guilt and particularly that of its ministers. Thus the renewal of the holiday hallowing starts with renewal of the preaching.

Jesus broke the Jewish laws concerning the Sabbath rest. He did it for the sake of the true hallowing of the Sabbath. The Sabbath is hallowed not by what men do or do not do, but by the action of Jesus Christ for the salvation of men. It was for this reason that the early Christian replaced the Sabbath by the resurrection day of Jesus Christ and called it "the Lord's Day." Hence Luther, giving not a literal but a spiritually interpreted translation of the Commandment, rightly renders the Hebrew word "Sabbath" with the German word for "holiday." Our Sunday is the day on which we let Jesus Christ deal with us and all men. To be sure, that should take place every day, but on Sunday we rest from our labor so that it may happen in a special way.

Sunday rest is the goal of hallowing Sunday. God desires to lead his people to their rest; he wants them to rest from the earthly workday. "Heart, rejoice; you shall be free from the misery of this earth and from the work of sin." So free from man's imperfect activity, the people of God are to behold and share in the completed, pure

66

work of God. The Christian who hallows the Sunday may experience Sunday rest as a reflection and promise of this eternal rest with the Creator and Redeemer and Perfecter of the world.

In the eyes of the world, Sunday points to the life of the children of God lived from his grace and to the summons of men to God's kingdom. So we pray, ''Thy kingdom come.''

SELECTED BIBLIOGRAPHY

WORKS OF BONHOEFFER

Act and Being. Tr. by Bernard Noble, with an Introduction by Ernst Wolf. New York: Harper & Brothers, 1962.

Christ the Center: A New Translation. New York: Harper & Row, 1978.

The Communion of Saints. Tr. by Ronald Gregor Smith and others. New York: Harper & Row, 1963. British edition entitled *Sanctorum Communio.* London: William Collins, 1963.

"Concerning the Christian Idea of God," *The Journal of Religion,* Vol. XII, No. 2 (April, 1932), pp. 177–185.

The Cost of Discipleship. Tr. by Reginald H. Fuller, with Memoir by G. Leibholz. New York: The Macmillan Co., First Edition, abridged, 1948; Second Edition, unabridged and revised, 1959; Paperback Edition, 1963.

Creation and Fall. Tr. by John C. Fletcher. New York: The Macmillan Co., 1959.

Ethics. Ed. by Eberhard Bethge. Tr. by Neville Horton Smith. New York: The Macmillan Co., 1955.

Gesammelte Schriften, I-IV. Ed. by Eberhard Bethge. Munich: Chr. Kaiser Verlag, 1958–1961. (Contains several writings in English.)

Letters and Papers from Prison. Ed. by Eberhard Bethge. Tr. by Reginald H. Fuller. London: SCM Press, First Edition, 1953; Second Edition, revised, 1956. American edition entitled *Prisoner for God.* New York: The Macmillan Co., 1954; Paperback Edition entitled *Letters and Papers from Prison,* 1962.

Life Together. Tr., with an Introduction, by John W. Doberstein. New York: Harper & Brothers, 1954.

No Rusty Swords. Cleveland: Collins-World, 1977.

Prayers from Prison, interpreted by J. C. Hampe. Philadelphia: Fortress Press, 1978.

Temptation. Tr. by Kathleen Downham. New York: The Macmillan Co., 1955.

The Way to Freedom. Cleveland: Collins-World, 1977.

WORKS ABOUT BONHOEFFER
Extended Treatments

Bailey, J. M. *The Steps of Bonhoeffer.* New York: The Macmillan Co., 1971.

Bethge, Eberhard. *Bonhoeffer: Exile and Martyr.* New York: Seabury Press, 1976.

_____. "The Challenge of Dietrich Bonhoeffer's Life and Theology," *The Chicago Theological Seminary Register,* Vol LI, No. 2 (February, 1961), pp. 1–38.

_____. *Dietrich Bonhoeffer.* New York: Harper & Row, 1977.

Godsey, John D. *The Theology of Dietrich Bonhoeffer.* Philadelphia: Westminster Press, 1960.

Marty, Martin E. (ed.) *The Place of Bonhoeffer.* New York: Association Press, 1962.

Shorter Essays and Related Works

Bell, G. K. A. *The Church and Humanity, 1939–1946,* especially Chapters XVIII and XX. London: Longmans, Green & Co., 1946.

_____. "The Church and the Resistance Movement in Germany," *The Wiener Library Bulletin,* Vol. XI, Nos. 3–4, pp. 21–23.

Berger, Peter L. "Camus, Bonhoeffer and the World Come of Age," *The Christian Century,* April 8 and 15, 1959.

_____. *The Precarious Vision,* especially Chapters 8 and 9. Garden City, N. Y.: Doubleday & Co., 1961.

Bethge, Eberhard. "Dietrich Bonhoeffer," *The Student Movement,* Vol. LVI, No. 3 (1954), pp. 24–26. The same article appeared in *Campus Lutheran,* Vol. VI, No. 3 (December, 1954), pp. 20–23.

_____. "Dietrich Bonhoeffer," in *German Life and Letters,* pp. 126–130. Oxford: Basil Blackwell, 1957. The same article appeared in *World Dominion,* Vol. XXXV, No. 2 (April, 1957), pp. 77–81.

_____. "Dietrich Bonhoeffer: An Account of His Life," *The Plough,* Vol. III, No. 2 (1955), pp. 35–42.

_____. "The Editing and Publishing of the Bonhoeffer Papers," *The Andover Newton Bulletin,* Vol. LII, No. 2 (December, 1959), pp. 1–24.

Busing, Paul. F. W. "Reminiscences of Finkenwalde," *The Christian Century* (September 20, 1961), pp. 1108–1111.

De Jong, Pieter, "Camus and Bonhoeffer on the Fall," *Canadian Journal of Theology,* Vol. VII, No. 4 (October, 1961), pp. 245–257.

Downing, F. Gerald. "Man's Coming of Age: Dietrich Bonhoeffer and Christianity Without Religion," *Prism,* No. 68 (December, 1962).

Ebeling, Gerhard. *Word and Faith,* especially Chapter IV, "The 'Non-religious Interpretation of Biblical Concepts'," and Chapter IX, "Dietrich Bonhoeffer." Philadelphia: Fortress Press, 1963.

Ebersole, Marc C. *Christian Faith and Man's Religion,* especially Chapter 3, "The Christian Faith Without Religion." New York: Thomas Y. Crowell Co., 1961.

Godsey, John D. "Barth and Bonhoeffer," *The Drew Gateway,* Vol. XXXIII, No 1 (Autumn, 1962), pp. 3–20.

_____. "Theology from a Prison Cell," *The Drew Gateway,* Vol. XXVII, No. 3 (Spring, 1957), pp. 139–154.

Green, Clifford. "Bonhoeffer's Concept of Religion," *Union Seminary Quarrterly Review,* Vol. XIX. No. 1 (November, 1963), pp. 11–12.

_____. *The Sociality of Christ and Humanity: Dietrich Bonhoeffer's Early Theology.* Roanoke, Va.: Scholars Press, 1975.

Hamilton, William. *The New Essence of Christianity.* New York: Association Press, 1961.

_____. "A Secular Theology for a World Come of Age," *Theology Today,* Vol. XVIII, No. 4 (January, 1962), pp. 435–459.

Hill, George G. "Bonhoeffer: Bridge Between Liberalism and Orthodoxy," *The New Christian Advocate* (June, 1957), pp. 80–83.

Hillerbrand, Hans J. "Dietrich Bonhoeffer and America," *Religion in Life,* Vol. XXX, No. 4 (Autumn, 1961), pp. 568–579.

Jenkins, Daniel. *Beyond Religion.* Philadelphia: Westminster Press, 1962.

Lehmann, Paul L. "Commentary: Dietrich Bonhoeffer in America," *Religion in Life,* Vol. XXX, No. 4 (Autumn, 1961), pp. 616–618.

Lochman, J. M. "From the Church to the World," in *New Theology No. 1,* ed. by Martin E. Marty and Dean G. Peerman, pp. 169–181. New York: The Macmillan Co., 1964.

Macquarrie, John. *Twentieth Century Religious Thought,* Chapter XX, 98, "A German Theologian: Dietrich Bonhoeffer." New York: Harper & Row, 1963.

Marty, Martin E. "Bonhoeffer: Seminarians' Theologian," *The Christian Century* (April 20, 1960), pp. 467–469.

Minthe, Eckhard. "Bonhoeffer's Influence in Germany," *The Andover Newton Quarterly,* New Series, Vol. II, No. 1 (September, 1961), pp. 13–45.

Niebuhr, Reinhold. "The Death of a Martyr," *Christianity and Crisis,* Vol. V, No. 11 (June 25, 1945), pp. 6–7.

Richmond, James. "Beyond All Reason," in *Four Anchors from the Stern,* ed. by Alan Richardson, pp. 36–46. London: SCM Press, 1963.

Roark, Dallas M. *Dietrich Bonhoeffer.* Makers of the Modern Theological Mind. Waco, Tex.: Word Books, 1972.

Robinson, John A. T. *Honest to God.* Philadelphia: Westminister Press, 1963.

Robinson, John A. T., and Edwards, David L. *The Honest to God Debate.* Philadelphia: Westminster Press, 1963.

Smith, Ronald Gregor. *The New Man,* especially Chapter V, "This-worldly Transcendence." New York: Harper & Brothers, 1956.

Student World, Vol. LVI, No. 1 (1963). (Special Issue on "Secularization.")

Van Buren, Paul M. *The Secular Meaning of the Gospel,* especially Chapter I, "Introduction." New York: The Macmillan Co., 1963.

Vidler, A. R. (ed.) *Soundings: Essays Concerning Christian Understanding,* Chapter 11, "Religion and the National Church." London: Cambridge University Press, 1962.

West, Charles C. *Communism and the Theologians: Study of an Encounter,* especially Chapter 7. London: SCM Press, 1958.

————. "Dietrich Bonhoeffer—The Theologian," *The Student Movement,* Vol. LVI, No. 3 (1954), pp. 27–29. The same article appeared in *Campus Lutheran,* Vol. VI, No. 3 (December, 1954), pp. 23–25.